Note

If you've ever been to a farm or a petting zoo—and even if you haven't—you're sure to recognize the animals pictured in this book. Here you can color and read about cattle, goats, sheep, horses, pigs, chickens and many other animals that provide us with so many of the things we need. You'll learn interesting facts about them too. So have fun visiting your farm animal friends!

Farm Animals
Coloring Book

Lisa Bonforte

DOVER PUBLICATIONS, INC.
Mineola, New York

Bibliographical Note

Farm Animals Coloring Book is a new work, first published by
Dover Publications, Inc., in 1997.

International Standard Book Number

ISBN-13: 978-0-486-29781-1
ISBN-10: 0-486-29781-0

Manufactured in the United States by Courier Corporation
29781009
www.doverpublications.com

"Welcome to the farm!"

Cattle are very important animals
on the farm. Cows are female cattle.

Cows eat grass and from
the grass make milk.

Cows provide us with
milk and meat.

Cows like to graze together.

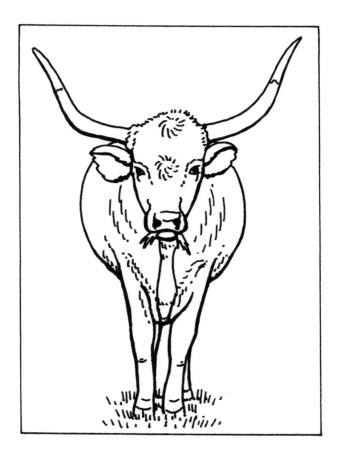

Male cattle are called
bulls or steers.

Both bulls and cows can have horns.

Newborn cattle are called calves.

At birth calves can weigh
from 50 to 100 pounds!

Cows are gentle and friendly animals.

Male goats are called billy goats.

Female goats are called nanny goats.

Nanny goats give milk that is
sweeter than cow's milk.

Goats are very sure-footed
and are good jumpers.

Goats eat many kinds of plants.
They'll even eat the bark of trees!

Male sheep are called rams. Rams
have horns that curve outward.

Female sheep are called ewes.

Sheep are important for
their meat and their wool.

Wool is sheared from sheep
to make warm clothing.

Sheep, like cattle, eat grass
and many other plants as well.

Sheep are timid animals and
always graze together in groups.

Baby sheep are called lambs.

Lambs are always born in the spring.

Lambs are frisky animals
who love to play.

They are ready to run and jump
just three weeks after they're born.

Male pigs are called boars.
Females are called sows.
Many weigh over 300 pounds!

Pigs are very clean animals, but in
warm weather they wallow in
the mud to keep cool.

Pigs eat corn, potatoes, barley,
fish meal and lots more.

A baby pig is called a piglet.

Three little piglets in the hay!

The male chicken is called a rooster.
The rooster crows loudly at dawn.

A female chicken is called a hen.
Chickens provide us with
meat and eggs.

Many roosters have bright
and colorful feathers.

Chickens spend the night in a hen
house, protected from animals like
foxes who might hunt them.

Hens sit on their eggs to keep them warm and help them hatch.

Chicks are baby chickens.

Chicks can run about and peck for food just one day after they're born!

Ducks are valued for their meat.
Their fluffy feathers are used
to fill the softest pillows.

Ducks lay up to sixteen eggs at a time.
The baby ducks are called ducklings.

Ducks eat grass and grain
and grow very quickly.

Ducks love the water and swim
very well with their webbed feet.

Geese are larger than ducks
and have longer necks.

When a goose is disturbed it raises
its head and honks loudly.

Geese graze on grass and also
search for food in the water.

Turkeys are large birds,
important for their meat.

The red pouch-like skin over a
turkey's throat is called a wattle.

When turkeys are frightened they huddle together and gobble loudly.

Rabbits are raised for their meat and fur.

Some rabbits are bred as pets.

Donkeys are strong and can
carry heavy loads.

Donkeys are also called burros and
in some places people ride them
like horses.

The mule is a cross between a
horse and a donkey.

The horse is one of the most
important animals on the farm.

Female horses are called mares;
males are called stallions or geldings.

Horses eat hay, oats and barley.

A baby horse is called a foal.

A foal can stand up and walk just
half an hour after it's born!

Horses have long legs
and are fast runners.

Collies are favorite farm dogs.
They help herd cattle and sheep.

There are kittens on the farm, too,
and like kittens everywhere,
they love to play!